STOICISM

Tackle life with courage, self-control, a sense of justice and wisdom by embracing the Stoic Philosophy of Life

by Wallace Foulds

Text Copyright © Wallace Foulds

Legal & Disclaimer

The information contained in this book is not designed to replace or take the place of any form of medicine or professional medical advice. The information in this book has been provided for educational and entertainment purposes only.

The information contained in this book has been compiled from sources deemed reliable, and it is accurate to the best of the Author's knowledge; however, the Author cannot guarantee its accuracy and validity and cannot be held liable for any errors or omissions. Changes are periodically made to this book. You must consult your doctor or get professional medical advice before using any of the suggested remedies, techniques, or information in this book.

Upon using the information contained in this book, you agree to hold harmless the Author from and against any damages, costs, and expenses, including any legal fees potentially resulting from the application of any of the information provided by this guide. This disclaimer applies to any damages or injury caused by the use and application, whether directly or indirectly, of any advice or information presented, whether for breach of contract, tort, negligence, personal injury, criminal intent, or under any other cause of action.

You agree to accept all risks of using the information presented inside this book. You need to consult a professional medical practitioner in order to ensure you are both able and healthy enough to participate in this program.

Table of Contents

Introduction

When we meet a person who never seems phased by life's ups and downs, we wonder how they remain so calm, so unflappable. Not only do they not seem phased by irritations, negativity, or even tragedy, they maintain the same equilibrium in times of great fortune and joy. Their reaction is equally implacable whether they have just been given a promotion or been retrenched.

What is their secret? Are they unfeeling? What mantras do they chant? Are they mentally on another planet? Chances are, you will hear people remarking, "He's a real stoic. Nothing ruffles his feathers.' What they are referring to is that these people are practising Stoicism, whereby the practitioner is no longer affected by life and all its follies and is instead guided by an inner wisdom and clear judgment.

A deceptively simple philosophy, Stoicism doesn't offer many teachings, but those teachings are powerful, simple and practical - meant to be applied and practised, not merely discussed. The crux of Stoicism is to better understand the world and our interactions within it so as to develop an inner peace to overcome adversity. A Stoic understands that life is finite, so he maximizes the time that's allotted to him to the fullest using self-control, logic, and forbearance.

Here, we will look into the origins of this powerful philosophy. We will examine how Stoicism was traditionally practised, and how its principles are still relevant in these modern times, if not even more so. Most importantly, we will take you through effective Stoic practices that you can apply to your everyday life to become someone who tackles life with courage, self-control, a sense of justice and wisdom.

Chapter 1:

What, When and Why?

Stoicism originated in Athens, early in the 3rd century BC. It was developed by Zeno of Citium as a melding of the prevailing philosophical teachings of Socrates, who taught that wisdom, courage, temperance and justice were the keys to fulfilment, and the Cynics, who promoted poverty and the rejection of material wealth.

Zeno upheld that virtue was the path to attain Eudaimonia - a life worth living. He taught that on this quest, a Stoic would meet "indifferents" - situations that would either positively or negatively affect one's pursuit of virtue - but that the Stoic would be ultimately indifferent to these situations, only seeing them as preferred (e.g. health, education, wealth) or dispreferred (e.g. illness, ignorance, poverty). The Stoic would even recognize that each situation had positive and negative influences on the attainment of virtue.

Zeno said that in order to arrive at this state of mind, the Stoic should examine 3 main areas of study.

The 3 Main Areas of Stoic Study in Ancient Times

1. Physics

Physics included the natural world, the universe and beyond, God, and the divine under the umbrella of reason. According to Zeno, everything was interconnected - there was no disparity between a flower and the most powerful of leaders; it all came to the same in the end.

2. Logic

Social sciences, psychology, history, sociology - all these fell under the umbrella of logic, which was prized by the ancient Stoics. Through epistemology, they examined the nature of knowledge and how to gain it, as well as the nature of truth, belief, and falsity and how to differentiate between them.

The Stoics used logic to investigate the nature of physics.

3. Ethics

The practical end of the investigation into the nature of physics was how to live with ethics and the recognition that only wisdom, courage, temperance and justice were purely good - everything else was an indifferent.

Chapter 2:

Who?

Then

Three Stoic practitioners stood out as leaders of the philosophy, and their writings and discourses are still quoted and turned to today. How have these three disparate men inspired presidents, writers, entrepreneurs, kings, artists, and countless others who go through life with an equilibrium born of a logical mind? What can they teach us, even in these modern and complicated times?

---

1. Marcus Aurelius (121 - 180 C.E.)

Marcus Aurelius, the great Roman emperor, took the time to record his reflections on compassion, restraint and humility while ruling over one of greatest ancient empires. He focused on turning the magnifying glass onto one's own perception and judgement of situations. He also advocated the need to develop a greater viewpoint, essentially, 'look at the bigger picture.' Finally, he upheld that philosophy should be applied in life, not just read about and discussed, and, most importantly, he practised what he preached:

"No-one could ever accuse you of being quick-witted.
All right, but there are plenty of other things you can't claim
you "haven't got in you." Practice the virtues you can show:
honesty, gravity, endurance, austerity, resignation,
abstinence, patience, sincerity, moderation, seriousness,
high-mindedness. Don't you see how much you have to offer -
beyond excuses like "can't"? And yet you still settle for less."
Meditations

2. Epictetus (A.D. 50 - 135)

Epictetus was born a slave, and rose above his suffering to found a school which inspired the crème de la crème of Greek intellectual society. Epictetus said that we would do well to remember that the ideas of attachment and ownership are mere illusions. A famous anecdote illustrates this lesson:

"I keep an iron lamp by the side of my household gods, and, on hearing a noise at the window, I ran down. I found that the lamp had been stolen. I reflected that the man who stole it was moved by no unreasonable motive. What then? Tomorrow, I say, you will find one of earthenware. Indeed, a man loses only that which he already has."

Epictetus did not actually write any of his teachings down, his teachings were recorded by a faithful student of his, Arrian.

3. Seneca (c. 4 B.C. - A.D. 65)

Seneca, advisor to a great emperor, only thought to comfort his loved ones when he was called upon by that emperor to commit suicide. Once lauded as one of the powerful men in ancient Rome, he nevertheless questioned the necessity of wealth and riches in order to live a 'good' life. Throughout his turbulent life, rising and falling from favour of the mighty, he maintained that the logical mind will conquer all, as one's perception of a situation is the only thing one can control, and that is the only thing that is required.

"For what prevents us from saying that the happy life is to have a mind that is free, lofty, fearless and steadfast - a mind that is places beyond the reach of fear, beyond the reach of desire, that counts virtue the only good, baseness the only evil, and all else but a worthless mass of things, which come and go without increasing or diminishing the highest good, and neither subtract any part from the happy life nor add any part to it?"
The Stoic Philosophy of Seneca: Essays and Letters

Now

The practice of Stoicism, powerful as it is, still resonates, even in these modern and complicated times, maybe more so. There are many important and successful people who still inculcate the ancient teachings to elevate them from ordinary to great.

Theodore Roosevelt - Epictetus and Aurelius accompanied the resilient Roosevelt on the almost-fatal 'River of Doubt' expedition.

George Washington - America's first president was lauded for his dignity, self-discipline and habit of doing the right thing, as illustrated in the famous cherry tree incident. He was guided towards Stoicism by friends in his younger years.

James Stockdale - Epictetus was the leading force for Stockdale's resilience during his time in Vietnam as a POW.

Wen Jiabao - How did Wen Jiabao lead China, the world's largest population, with his characteristic strength of mind? He has stated that he has read Aurelius' *Medidtations* more than 100 times.

Arnold Schwarzenegger - Heavyweight champion, famous actor and ex-Governor of California, Schwarzenegger is fuelled by the driving force of Stoicism.

Tim Ferriss - Ferriss is one of the most well-known followers of Stoicism. The angel investor, author and podcast host published Seneca's letters on a high-popular audiobook, *The Tao of Seneca*.

Jack Dorsey - The Co-founder of Twitter has also mentioned that he adheres to the Stoic philosophy.

Ralph Waldo Emerson - Emerson is well-known for how he inculcated Stoicism into his life and writing.

JK Rowling - The creator of a certain troubled young wizard is fuelled by Aurelius' teachings in her daily life.

Robert Greene - Greene, the prolific NLP author, has called Stoicism 'a beautiful philosophy'.

Anna Kendrick - Accomplished singer, actress and author Kendrick finds comfort in Aurelius' words.

Tom HIddleston - The 'Thor' actor pushes himself professionally and personally by remembering the writings of Seneca in *On the Shortness of Life*.

LL Cool J - Ryan Holiday's *The Obstacle Is the Way* is LL Cool J's go-to inspirational book.

T-Pain - T-Pain has won a Grammy and reached Platinum sales of his album, and he shows his admiration of Stoic philosophy by recording the 'Stoic' mix-tape and producing an album entitled 'Stoicville'.

Follow us as we explore how Stoicism can also set you on a path to a better state of mind to elevate your personal life, your career and your spiritual path. Examine how Stoic principles can help you let go of your reliance on your reflexive senses and impulses, and free your mind to use logic and reason as the rudders to steer you through a life worth living.

Chapter 3:

It's All In The Mind

Mind Before Matter

"You have the power of your mind - not <u>outside events</u>. Realise this, and you will find strength."
Marcus Aurelius, <u>Meditations</u>

We have no control over what happens to us whether we analyse, agonise or relax, so we might as well relax and take things as they come.

This isn't easy since we have an inherent fear of the idea of a lack of control. We want to think that we have some kind of control over situations, so we strain to keep it. When we ultimately realise we have no control, we react with emotion and allow it to affect us.

Scenario 1

A high school girl runs for class president. She has worked very hard to gain the trust of her classmates and is the frontrunner for the title, but her rival launches a smear campaign against her, saying that she isn't true to her word and has her own agenda. She is stung by the accusations and agonizes over them, losing sleep and her focus. Eventually, she drops out of the race.

Scenario 2

A man is standing in line waiting for his morning coffee. Another man rushes in and cuts in front of him without a word of apology. The man has a choice - he can choose to be angry at the slight, or he can choose to be gracious about it and let it go. He chooses to not let the situation affect him and just smiles at the other customers who are watching how he would react. When it finally comes to the man's turn, the barista gives him an extra coffee for being so calm.

The Stoic Solution

A Stoic always keeps in mind that life is full of millions of variables over which we have zero control. We can only influence one variable in the equation: how we react to situations.

In the first situation outlined above, the girl a chose to react with emotion, and this adversely affected her. The man in the second situation chose to be Stoic about his setback and he reacted with tranquillity -he let the setback slide off his back as water would slide off a duck's back.

The way to this tranquillity is through virtue, using reason and logic to work through the emotions. Remember that the only thing we can control is our mind, so we'd better use it to its full potential. Consider how Buddha defeated Mara:

Buddha and Mara

Mara, wanting to destroy Buddha, sent an army to fight him. First, they threw flaming rocks, but the flaming rocks transformed into flowers as they neared Buddha. Then, they shot arrows at Buddha, but even they turned into flowers and didn't injure him. Try as he might, Mara couldn't defeat Buddha because Buddha had not allowed external attacks to invade his inner peace.

Tied To The Back Of A Cart

The Animal And The Cart

An animal is tied to the back of a moving cart. How can he be happy as he's forced to move when the cart moves, and stop when the cart stops? He has to learn to accept his fate and just follow along with a positive attitude.

A Stoic must accept that things are how they are. We are all bound to fate, things will happen as they are meant to happen. Understanding where we stand in nature frees us to move on with life.

In the famous analogy above, the animal is the human being and the cart is fate. Fate moves inexorably forward whether we want it to or not, and we are bound to it for better or for worse. Since we, like the animal, are already stuck in a situation, struggling won't help; it may even make the situation worse.

Scenario 1

A man is devastated that he's lost his job. Instead of accepting what has happened, he spends his days hashing and rehashing what went wrong and it drives him to drink. One day, he meets a man in a bar and they get to talking about his industry. It turns out that the man he has met is actually looking for someone of his expertise and is considering hiring him, but when he sees the man's negative attitude, he reconsiders.

Scenario 2

A lady is diagnosed with terminal cancer and is told she has only a few months left to live. She doesn't allow this to bring her down. Instead, she chooses to wrap up her affairs so that her children are taken care of. Then she starts to tick off her bucket list to make sure she is as fulfilled as possible when the time comes.

The Stoic Solution

A Stoic understands that only when we stop struggling with fate can we open up to the positive side of things, and even see opportunities that might come our way; just as when the animal starts to relax, it will have less of a hard time. It might even benefit from its situation - perhaps it is pulled through beautiful scenery that it might never have ventured through itself ... or people feel sorry for it, so they throw it food to eat.

In scenario one, the man can't accept the hand that fate has dealt him, so he remains in a negative frame of mind about it instead of accepting it and moving on. He, therefore, loses out on opportunities that come his way. The lady in the second scenario, on the other hand, understands that 'that's just life'.

She just accepts the situation and makes the best of it that she could.

Again, the way to this acceptance is by logically working through it with our Nature-given mind. Recognise that nature will run its course no matter how we try to take control, so we might as well stop fighting it and, as they say, 'go with the flow'.

"Do not ask things to happen as you wish, but wish them to happen as they do, and your life will go smoothly."
Epictetus, *The Discourses*

Reason It Out

"Everything - a horse, a vine - is created for some duty. Man's true delight is to do the things he was made for."
Marcus Aurelius, *Meditations*

The Stoics refer to a being's Oikeiosis - house or orientation - as being the one thing that they were placed here on Earth to do. Every living being has an Oikeiosis. A sheep's Oikeiosis is to eat, sleep and reproduce. A flower's Oikeiosis is to photosynthesize, grow and release its pollen.

A human being's Oikeiosis, according to the Stoics, is to survive much as other animals are meant to, but we were given a higher purpose - to use reason to guide our lives. Being blessed with the ability to use logic and ethics, it is our natural state to always be guided by them in our daily lives, and not by our emotions, moods and desires.

Scenario 1

A girl has an assignment to do, which she has been given ample time to complete. Instead of allocating time daily to complete the task, she chooses to play a computer game at every free moment. She leaves it to the night before to rush to complete the assignment, so in the end, she doesn't get to sleep that night. She is exhausted the next morning.

Scenario 2

A man is tempted to have an affair with a lady at his office. She sends him signals like touching his hand when he passes her something and has even volunteered to accompany him on business trips. As tempted as he is to stray, he loves his wife and children and he knows that indulging in his desires will break up their happy home. In the end, he decides to transfer to another branch to avoid the lady altogether.

The Stoic Solution

Both the man and the girl in the above scenarios were tasked with either using their logic and reason to guide their actions or following their moods and desires.

The girl succumbed to her desires, what made her feel happy at that moment, rather than reasoning with herself that the right thing to do would be to give the assignment ample time so that she could produce a quality piece of work.

The man, on the other hand, resisted his desires and used reason and logic to steer him onto the right path. He remembered his purpose in life as a husband and a father and based his actions on that purpose. He followed his Oikeiosis.

The Stoic will always strive to follow their Oikeiosis as the man did, and reason with them self when their desires threaten to overtake logic.

"Were I a nightingale, I would act the part of a nightingale; were I a swan, the part of a swan."
Epictetus, Discourses

Chapter 4:

It's All In The Perception

Neither Good, nor Bad

Death and life, honour and dishonour, pain and pleasure - all these things equally happen to good men and bad, being things which make us neither better nor worse. Therefore they are neither good nor evil.
Marcus Aurelius, <u>Meditations</u>

According to Plato, a purely GOOD thing could never have a negative outcome. Stoic philosophers believed that only 4 things were purely GOOD: courage, self-control, a sense of justice and wisdom. All other things were INDIFFERENTS - a Stoic practitioner would not be affected by them either way. All a Stoic could say about indifferents was whether they were preferred indifferents, or dispreferred indifferents.

Preferred indifferents would typically be things like good health, good wealth, or knowledge. These things, while they seem good to us, are only preferred indifferents to the Stoic's way of thinking because they are only as good as the thing they are benefitting. It's all a matter of context.

Likewise, dispreferred indifferents like illness, poverty and ignorance are not typically what one would appreciate, but they might benefit in other ways when all the weighing and checking is done.

Scenario 1

A man is struggling to make ends meet (dispreferred). One day, his wealthy aunt passes away (dispreferred) and leaves him with the bulk of her fortune (preferred). Now he can afford a better lifestyle (preferred) but he and his family come to expect more and more and are not satisfied with what they have (dispreferred), whereas when they were not well off, they were grateful for what they had and never craved for more (preferred).

Scenario 2

A lady has suffered from a chronic illness for a long time (dispreferred). She has spent most of her savings on medical treatments (dispreferred), and has lost her job (dispreferred). She meets a lady who introduces her to an alternative form of treatment which is cost effective (preferred). She follows the treatment religiously and regains her health (preferred) and becomes an advocate for the treatment, earning money by giving talks and spreading the word about the treatment (preferred).

The Stoic Solution

A situation cannot be purely good or bad; it's really up to us how we wish to perceive the situation and what we make of it. The man in scenario 1 finally had a preferred indifferent come his way, but he squandered the opportunity and turned it into a dispreferred indifferent by not using reason to think through his materialistic wants.

The woman in scenario 2, on the other hand, recognised the chance that she was given and transformed the preferred indifferents that came her way into more preferred situations, even benefitting others with her own good fortune.

"The universe is change; our life is what our thoughts make it."
Marcus Aurelius, *Meditations*

This, Too, Shall Pass

"Look back over the past, with its changing empires that rose and fell, and you can foresee the future, too."
Marcus Aurelius, *Meditations*

Life is ephemeral - that is what the Stoics always kept in the forefront of their meditations. Whatever trials and tribulations came their way, they did not let them affect their happiness because they knew that it was only temporary. Conversely, they also didn't allow good news or fortune to affect them, because they knew that those things, too, were only theirs for a fleeting moment.

Scenario 1

A young man is accepted into a good job. He is so happy, he proposes to his girlfriend, who accepts. The young man is over the moon; he feels as if he is on a roll and that nothing can bring him down. Several months down the line, his company faces bankruptcy and he, being the newest member of its staff, is retrenched. He goes into an emotional tailspin which his fiancé cannot cope with, and she leaves him.

Scenario 2

After months of searching, a lady is happy to have finally found an apartment that fits all her criteria. She makes an offer to buy, it and the owner verbally agrees to the offered price. However, as she is in the midst of applying for a loan, she is told that the owner has changed his mind and has rented the apartment out. Although she is a little disappointed that she has lost out, she knows that another apartment will come along in time. She rationalises that now she knows the location she wants to buy in, and can save up and work towards being in a more comfortable financial situation.

The Stoic Solution

The young man in the first scenario allowed circumstances to dictate his emotions, and therefore his actions. A Stoic would always keep in mind that things come, and things go, but what remains constant is our ability analyse the situation logically and react to them however we wish to.

Although the lady in the second scenario faced a setback in her pursuit of something she had set her sights on, she remained level-headed and moved on from the disappointment.

"Time is a sort of river of passing events, and strong is its current; no sooner is a thing brought to sight than it is swept by and another takes its place, and this too will be swept away."
Marcus Aurelius, Meditations

Life Is Not Too Short

"That which Fortune has not given, she cannot take away."
Seneca, Agamemnon

In his treatise called "On the Shortness of Life", Seneca says that it's not that life is too short; it's that we squander what life we are given to live by agonising about it instead of living it.

Fear of the unknown can breed anxiety, which holds us back from carrying out our true life's purpose. Once the thing we fear becomes known, for the most part, it is rarely as bad as it seemed in our own tortured minds.

The Condemned Prisoner

A prisoner has been locked up for many years, and finally, his death sentence is passed down. When the guards arrive at his cell to take him to his execution, they find him relaxing and playing a game with his warden. As they start dragging the prisoner away, he says, "You are my witnesses! I was up by one piece there! I beat him!"

Scenario 2

A man's friend suddenly passes away of a heart attack. The man starts to worry about his own health and starts to eat better and exercise. He stops smoking and drinking, and his health improves. As time goes by, however, he still feels he's not doing enough. He exercises more and more every day and eats less and less. Eventually, he collapses.

The Stoic Solution

Stoic philosophers remind us that we were never guaranteed life in the first place, so what's the point of worrying about when it will be taken away from us? The prisoner in the Stoic anecdote knew how to always focus on positive things, even to the very last minute of his life. The same goes for the lady in the scenario given two chapters ago; she knew she only had a finite amount of days to live, so she prioritised what was important to her and worked towards it.

In the second scenario, while the man started off doing something positive by taking better care of himself, he became too obsessed with an outcome which was always going to be inevitable anyway. While it is healthy to be aware of the inevitable end, which we will address a little later in this book, it doesn't serve our purpose to become fearful of it and lead our lives according to that fear.

If we use our rational mind to consider it, we would realise that yes, it will happen, so what can I do to maximise my time here on Earth before it happens?

"You live as if you were destined to live forever, no thought of your frailty ever enters your head, of how much time has already gone by you take no heed. You squander time as if you drew from a full and abundant supply, though all the while that day which you bestow on some person or thing is perhaps your last."
Seneca, <u>On The Shortness Of Life</u>

Time Is Precious

"Drink and be merry for when you're dead you will look like this."
Montaigne

In the midst of celebrations, politician & essayist Montaigne would every so often hold up a painting of a corpse in a coffin and toast his friends with this grounding statement. He was reminding them that the time we have on this earth is finite, so we'd better make the most of every moment we have.

While we shouldn't obsess about the finite nature of Life, we should always remember that it IS finite and we only have these few years to live our lives to the fullest.

Scenario 1

A young executive works and works, thinking to build a fortune for her family. Meanwhile, her family never sees her and her husband feels more and more distant from her every day. Her children grow up not really knowing their mother. Eventually, when she retires, she finds that she has nothing emotional to connect her with her husband or children.

Scenario 2

A nurse who works on hourly shifts still finds the time to cook for his family every night and makes sure the children are well taken care of. On the weekends, he helps out at the homeless shelter and also mentors underprivileged teens, bringing his children along too, when appropriate.

The Stoic Solution

In both scenarios, the nurse and the executive are given the same amount of hours in a day. It's how they choose to spend those hours that makes the difference. Once you realise this, you will seek to improve the quality of your life, as opposed to being bogged down by the unimportant.

"Execute every act of thy life as though it were thy last."
Marcus Aurelius, Meditations

Failure Is Not The End

"Does what's happened keep you from acting with justice, generosity, self-control, sanity, prudence, honesty, humility, straightforwardness, and all other qualities that allow a person's nature to fulfil itself? So remember this principle when something threatens to cause you pain: the thing itself was no misfortune at all; to endure it and prevail is great good fortune."
Marcus Aurelius, <u>Meditations</u>

We put ourselves out there everyday, and we expect recognition, if not accolades. Unfortunately the world is indifferent to us and our achievements, and we should recognise this fact.

Scenario 1

A fresh advertising executive completes his first presentation for a campaign. He is very excited about his work as he is passionate about the subject, and has put all his energy and time into it.

At the client presentation, the executive is nonplussed that the client does not immediately indicate their approval. A few days later, the client reverts that the presentation is not going in the direction that they are looking for. The executive is devastated and cannot accept the fact that something he was so passionate about has been rejected.

Scenario 2

A man has admired a woman from afar for a long time. One day, he finally gets up the courage to ask her out, but she says no. The man decides that he has wanted to be with her for too long now to quit, so he decides to be her friend and find out why she said no. He finds out that when he had first approached the lady, she had just broken up with her boyfriend. Several months later, the woman finally feels comfortable enough with him and agrees to date him.

The Stoic Solution

The account executive in the first scenario would do well to remember that failure is not the end of the line, it is, in fact, just a tool with which to practise to improve. A Stoic learns from their failure and setbacks, and through this learning comes growth, and eventually success.

The man in the second scenario recognised this and didn't give up at the first failing. Instead, he figured out what it took to succeed in what he wanted, and grew from his experience.

"The impediment to action advances action. What stands in the way becomes the way."
Marcus Aurelius, Meditations

Material Wealth Is Immaterial

"Wealth consists not in having great possessions, but in having few wants."
Epictetus, Discourses

The modern mind-set is that what we have is never enough. We are always yearning for more, the improved, the latest. The more desires are fulfilled, the more desires sprout up like weeds in an unkempt garden. What we don't realise is that while we are busy keeping up with the Jones' (or, nowadays, the Kardashians), they themselves are probably no happier than we are, regardless of what they seem have over us.

Scenario 1

Two neighbours are constantly at 'war' with each other over who has the most well-renovated house, the most beautifully-kept garden, and the flashiest car. It has reached a point where the once-friends barely even speak anymore, except to put each other down. Eventually, the tension becomes so hostile that one of them has to move away.

Scenario 2

A young woman from humble beginnings finally lands a good job, and she can finally afford what she could never have before. Instead of going for the flashiest car and the most upmarket condo, she invests her money wisely. She is not swayed by what her peers are buying, driving or wearing, sticking to what she is comfortable with. By the time she retires, she has saved up more than enough money to get her through her golden years.

The Stoic Solution

In the first scenario, the two friends allowed their attachment to material objects to overtake their reason and their innate sense of virtue. In the end, it even overshadowed their friendship. If they had acted with logic rather than pride, they would have seen that material objects are nothing compared to good relationships.

In the second scenario, the young woman continued her life with a level head despite all the temptations and peer pressure to upgrade, consume and accumulate. In the end, her level-headedness was rewarded by a comfortable retirement.

Strive to want less, not have more. Rationalise with yourself about every single purchase you intend to make. Will it help me to lead a more virtuous life, or will it distract me from my true purpose in life? Does my material body really need it, or is it a dispensable want?

"Wealth is the slave of a wise man. The master of a fool."
Seneca, Moral Essays, Volume I

Chapter 5:

Out With The Emotions

All Emotions Are Mine, I Can Do What I Want Them

"Today I escaped anxiety. Or no, I discarded it, because it was within me, in my own perceptions - not outside."
Marcus Aurelius, <u>Meditations</u>

As we saw earlier, no outside force is controlling our actions, reactions, and emotions. Much as it's easier to place responsibility on things outside of ourselves, a full laundry basket or overflowing inbox aren't, in themselves, stressful. How we react to something is completely up to us.

Scenario 1

A writer who has enjoyed past success finds himself sitting in front of his blank word processor day after day. As the days go past, he finds his heart speeding up at the thought of facing an upcoming deadline with nothing to show for it. As the anxiety mounts, his inspiration to write floats ever further away and he falls into despair.

> ### Scenario 2
>
> A lady is in a rush to get to an appointment. As she is driving, a car suddenly swerves into her lane, nearly causing her to hit it. Although shaken by the incident, she remains calm and brushes it off. To make things worse, she finds herself stuck at every red light along the way. Despite all these incidents that could potentially rile her up, she maintains her equilibrium and arrives cool and collected to have a very productive meeting.

The Stoic Solution

The author in the first scenario allowed his perception of the situation to cloud his thinking and, ultimately, affect his work. Instead of allowing his mind to mull over his past successes and fret over the possibility that he may not be able to replicate them, he would have done better to flip the situation around and focus on what would happen when he produced another best-seller.

It all comes from our own amazing mind that can use logic to reason things out. The lady in the second scenario was logical and understood that reacting angrily or in a harried manner would not have gotten her to her appointment any faster - in fact, it might have caused an accident. Additionally, she realises that if she'd arrived at the appointment in a harried state, she may not have been able to make such a good impression.

"The happiness of your life depends upon the quality of your thoughts: therefore, guard accordingly, and take care that you entertain no notions unsuitable to virtue and reasonable nature."
Marcus Aurelius, Meditations

On Emotion

Humans are blessed with the ability to experience and feel - but is it really a blessing? Emotions are reactions to what occurs to us, which we can't control. Are we to be reeds - blown in this direction or that by every gust of wind?

Seneca says that the idea of 'moderate emotions' is impractical because emotions are inherently irrational. Since we are also blessed with a higher mind that is able to dissect situations and use logic to create reason out of the seeming chaos, we can operate in a logical way that propels us forwards instead of backwards. The Stoics ask - shouldn't we use this Nature-given gift of reason to deal with the roiling emotions that surface every minute of our lives?

Here are a few practical ways to conquer those monkey emotions:

Logic Rules - Stoicism states that negative emotions cloud our judgement and cause us to react in ways that will turn out leading us away from the true path. We have to always remember that emotions tend to be illogical responses, so we should use logic to counter them.

Examine Your Biases - If you insist there is only one way to do things or live, you're bound to experience negative emotions when those biases are challenged. Have a look at your biases and open your mind to see that there are many ways to approach life.

Minimise The Negative - Stoicism doesn't aim to eradicate all emotion but to minimise negative emotion. Negative emotions like anger, sadness, envy and fear are what blocks us from being our best and real selves, so be conscious of those moments when you sense these emotions well up and work to quickly minimise them.

Maximize The Positive - While you shouldn't let them overtake your sense of reason, positive emotions are preferred over negative emotions. Allow them to permeate your mind, but remember that reason comes before mindless positivity.

Right Here And Now - Appreciate what you have right here and now and you will always find something positive about any situation. Stay in the now, not the past, nor the future.

What A Beautiful World - To practise appreciating what you have, start by appreciating the physical world around you. Open your eyes to how awe-inspiring it all is ... the dewy stillness of the early morning, the majestic mountains, or the mysterious sea.

Internalize - Practise keeping your emotions under wraps and not allowing them to show outwardly. One way to cultivate this habit is by watching emotional shows that would normally affect you. Acknowledge the emotions that rise up, but train yourself to not act on them (cry, shout, laugh).

Body Language - In a situation that would normally cause you to react emotionally, control your physical reactions - if you are provoked to get angry, resist the urge to frown or clench your fists. If you are told good news, don't let fly with a happy shout, fist pump, or even a smile.

Divert - Divert yourself by thinking of something else. Focus on singing a song in your head.

Save It For Later - Contrary to popular belief, Stoics don't aim to erase their emotions, rather to not place importance on them. Initially, however, there has to be a healthy outlet for those emotions, as suppressed emotions are not healthy. Make sure you find a safe outlet for your emotions, whether it be bashing a pillow in the privacy of your own bedroom, or writing in a journal.

Be Less Verbal - Minimise speaking in general. Instead, use the opportunity to observe and listen to things and people around you to get a clearer picture of the situation.

Respond Sparsely - When called upon to speak, weigh your answers and choose to respond as sparsely as possible. This will allow you to shelter your responses, and focus on working through them.

Don't Volunteer - Avoid sharing information about yourself, your feelings and your thoughts.

Avoid Complaining - When you complain, you are acknowledging that there is internal disturbance. Half the battle of conquering something is to not give voice to it in the first place.

Happy From The Heart

"Sick and yet happy, in peril and yet happy, dying and yet happy, in exile and happy, in disgrace and happy."
Epictetus, *Discourses*

Now that we have accepted that our happiness is generated by us, not outside factors, we should always be cheerful and positive. We should revel in what is here and now, and not worry about the past or yearn for more in the future.

Scenario 1

After many years of work with his company, a man has reached retirement age. His company is throwing him a retirement party and his wife has booked them onto a cruise around the world. At the party, he seems distant and doesn't seem to be enjoying himself. When his colleagues ask him why he tells them he is worried about the future. His colleagues remind him of how diligently he's been saving and how he has a tidy little retirement nest egg, but it doesn't stop him from worrying. Consequently he doesn't even enjoy his cruise.

Scenario 2

A girl is due for quite a serious surgery. She has been in the hospital for the past few days for monitoring and she is missing out on her best friend's 16th birthday. She is not down, however, and she keeps herself occupied by making sweet gifts for her friend. She has a smile and a kind word for everyone who comes to tend to her and visit her.

The Stoic Solution

When we worry and fret, we miss out on enjoying what we have right in front of us, as the man in the first scenario did. Instead of appreciating the love and admiration of his colleagues and wife and enjoying his hard-earned vacation, he chose to focus on the potentially negative outcome of his situation.

The girl in scenario 2, on the other hand, chose to focus on being positive because she had accepted the inevitability of her situation. In being positive, she not only made things better for herself, but for the people around her. They, in turn, returned the positivity to her.

"A man thus grounded must, whether he wills or not, necessarily be attended by constant cheerfulness and a joy that is deep and issues from deep within, since he finds delight in his own resources, and desires no joys greater than his inner joys."
Seneca, *The Stoic Philosophy of Seneca: Essays and Letters*

Anger Is A Choice

"He who has injured thee was either stronger or weaker than thee. If weaker, spare him; if stronger, spare thyself."
Seneca, *On Anger*

Detractors of Stoic philosophy say that anger is a reflex reaction, not a conscious choice, but Seneca says that this is not true. In his treatise, "On Anger", he details exactly what occurs when someone is upset. In what seems like an instant, we actually go through four stages before real anger sets in. Take the following scenario:

The 4 Stages Of Anger

A man gets to his parking space in an open-air car park to find that his car is not there.

Stage 1: Realisation - The man realises that his car is not where he left it. He searches around, just in case he didn't remember correctly, but can't find it.

Stage 2: Indignation - The man starts to feel indignant: "How DARE they!?!?"

Stage 3: Condemnation - The man comes up with all sorts of ways to pay the thief back for the theft: "Oooooh ... I'll show him!!"

Stage 4: Retribution - The man kicks a lamp post and calls the police.

The Stoic Solution

To Seneca, anger is therefore not a reflexive reaction like shivering in the cold or jumping at being startled. He argues that at any one of the 4 stages of anger, a logical mind could and should intervene and ask itself what is the most productive way forward.

"Anger, if not restrained, is frequently more hurtful to us than the injury that provokes it."
Seneca, *On Anger*

Chapter 6:

And ... Action!

Read With A Purpose

"Don't just say you have read books. Show that through them you have learned to think better, to be a more discriminating and reflective person. Books are the training weight of the mind. They are very helpful, but it would be a bad mistake to suppose that one has made progress simply by having internalized their contents."
Epictetus, <u>The Art of Living</u>

You can gather all the tools you like, but if you don't use them, they're worth nothing. So it is with reading.

Reading helps you to cultivate a well-rounded way of thinking and gain information, but it's what you do with these tools that make them special.

Scenario 1

After reading a particularly inspiring self-help book a man is fired-up to change his life. He starts looking for more inspiration in other books, interviews and even attends self-help courses to gather more and more tools to transform his life. He is excited to share his knowledge with his friends and family ... but they don't see him actually showing any changes in the way he talks, thinks or acts. He gets irate that they don't seem to be as excited as he is about his 'life transformation'.

Scenario 2

After reading a book given to her by a friend, a woman starts to view life differently. She writes down the key points that speak to her the most and ponders over how they could apply to her life. She then diligently analyses situations in her daily life to see if she can apply her new-found perspectives to them. Slowly, with diligence and effort, her attitude towards life changes, changing the way she speaks, reacts to and does things, and people around her notice that she's a lot calmer, more logical and proactive. They, in turn, are positively affected by her.

The Stoic Solution

As Epictetus advised, internalize the contents of books that you've read then apply them in your everyday life.

In the first scenario, the man was inspired by what he had read, which is the first step. Instead of immediately looking for ways to apply what he had learned, however, he kept gathering knowledge and sharing it. In the end, all the inspiration that he gathered was not used, so, in effect, wasted.

The woman in the second scenario took the advice that inspired her and immediately applied it to her life. She and those around her, therefore, saw the results and reaped the benefits of a transformed life.

Be aware of what books you read, as well, as Seneca advises, and choose those that give you practical advice which can be immediately applied.

"We should hunt out the helpful pieces of teaching and the spirited and noble-minded sayings which are capable of immediate practical application - not far far-fetched or archaic expressions or extravagant metaphors and figures of speech - and learn them so well that words become works."
Seneca, <u>Letters From a Stoic</u>

What Do You Spend Your Time On?

"A key point to bear in mind: The value of attentiveness varies in proportion to its object. You're better off not giving the small things more time than they deserve."
Marcus Aurelius, <u>Meditations</u>

You only have so much time at your disposal, so why waste it on the small stuff? Master the art of prioritising and you will excel in whatever you do.

Scenario 1

A working mother comes home from the office and sees that the house needs tending to. She also has to prepare the lunches for her children to bring to school the next morning, and complete some office work. She chooses to tidy up the house but then is too tired to do more than put together a few sandwiches and cut some fruits for the lunches. She goes to bed worrying about the office work that she will have to tackle early in the morning before sending her children to school.

Scenario 2

A woman at work has a pile of documents to tend to in her inbox. She also has an urgent deadline on a project. Her boss calls to request for her help to organise a last-minute dinner party.

Instead of choosing the easiest task to complete first, the woman spends a few moments to decide which task is most urgent. She quickly shuffles through the inbox tray to see if there are any documents that need to be tended to in the next 2 hours. After quickly dealing with the urgent documents, she spends 10 minutes to list down what she needs to do for the dinner party. Again, she tends to the tasks that can quickly and easily be done.

The woman then puts the rest of the documents and the dinner party out of her mind for 2 hours and focuses on completing the project. At the 2 hour mark, she leaves the project work for 10 minutes to tend to a few more items in her inbox and on her to-do list.

The Stoic Solution

The woman in the first scenario quickly chose to tackle the mindless but physically exhausting work of tidying up first. She tired herself out and didn't have the physical or mental energy to complete her other two tasks which were actually more pressing and time-reliant.

The woman at the office spent some time planning her course of action to not only tackle the more pertinent tasks on her list but use her mental and physical energy wisely. She gave everything a time frame and stuck to it. She quickly completed whatever tasks she could on the less mentally taxing things on her to-do list. Then she devoted her mental energy to working on the project, taking a time-allotted break from it to tackle the less mentally taxing tasks.

You can also schedule time for fun breaks, like watching a bit of television, reading a book or playing with your children, but set a time limit on them so that you are reminded of when to get back to the task at hand.

"Stop wandering about! You aren't likely to read your own notebooks, or ancient histories, or the anthologies you've collected to enjoy in your old age. Get busy with life's purpose, toss aside empty hopes, get active in your own rescue - if you care for yourself at all - and do it while you can."
Marcus Aurelius, Meditations

Dig Below The Surface

"A consciousness of wrongdoing is the first step to salvation."
This remark of Epicurus' is to me a very good one. For a person who is not aware that he is doing anything wrong has

*no desire to be put right. You have to catch yourself doing it
before you can reform.*
Seneca, Letters From a Stoic

The first step towards change is recognition for the need of it.
Look deep into yourself and ask what causes you to stray away
from the logical, right path.

Scenario 1

A couple get into an argument and they start to accuse each
other of perceived wrong-doings in the past. The woman
accuses the man of never thinking about her needs and
feelings. The man counter attacks with the accusation that she
never expresses herself and makes him guess what she wants.
Tensions rise and they end up sleeping apart. The next
morning, the woman sits the man down and apologises, telling
him that she did a lot of thinking over what he said and that
he's right, she does need to communicate better if she wants
things a certain way.

Scenario 2

A woman is saving her money to buy a house. She is well on
her way to being able to secure a down-payment on a decent
property. She meets a friend who tells her about a business
opportunity that could help her achieve her financial goals
faster, and it sounds very convincing, especially since her
friend says that she benefitted from it. The woman is
convinced and jumps right in, thinking that although she is
not very confident in her ability to market the business, she
can learn along the way. Eventually, after nearly a year of
trying but not having the time to learn up the marketing
techniques, she is nowhere near recovering her substantial
investment.

The Stoic Solution

Scenario 1 showed a woman who took an objective look within and was honest with herself about where she could improve. She took it a step further and vocalised her shortcomings, and took immediate steps to rectify the issue. Then she worked on herself to change the undesirable trait.

The woman in scenario 2, on the other hand, was not honest with herself about her capabilities, inclinations or the time she had available to do what needed to be done. She forged on, hoping that everything would fall into place while she didn't address the biggest obstacle in the way of success - her lack of knowledge of the business.

Some people boast about their failings: can you imagine someone who counts his faults as merits without ever giving thought to their cure? So - to the best of your ability - demonstrate your own guilt, conduct inquiries of your own into all the evidence against yourself. Play the first part of prosecutor, then of judge and finally of pleader in mitigation. Be harsh with yourself at times."
Seneca, *Letters From a Stoic*

Right Here And Now

"True happiness is to understand our duties toward God and man. To enjoy the present, without anxious dependence on the future."
Seneca, *Letters From a Stoic*

We've lost touch with many things in the modern age, especially the ability to be present and connect with our surroundings, events, companions, and even ourselves.

Scenario 1

A woman feels she has no time for herself, so in between tasks she unwinds by using her phone; either messaging people or playing games. She even uses her phone constantly when her daughter is around. One day, her daughter tells her, "Mummy, please put the phone down and play with me." Only then does the woman realise that although she's physically with her daughter, she is not mentally or emotionally with her.

Scenario 2

A man meets a lady who seems to be the perfect match for him. They date for over a year, and he feels he is ready to propose to her. He is stunned when she turns him down. The couple cannot get past this, so they part ways. The man is even more stunned when, several months later, he learns that the lady has settled down with her new boyfriend. He asks her why she refused his proposal, but decided to settle with the other man, and is told that the other man is always present; with her, with his work, in whatever he is doing. He pays full attention to one thing before moving on to the next.

The Stoic Solution

The lady in the first scenario would have done well to focus on the present. When she was with her daughter, she should have focused on her daughter, talking and listening only to her, at least for a little while. Her daughter would then have felt appreciated, as the lady in the second scenario felt with her new husband.

Wherever you are, and whomever you're with, being present improves your quality of life. At dinner, put down your phone and talk to your companions. Taste and savour your food. Allow the background music to wash over you. At work, focus on the task at hand, and only that. Pay attention to its details and carry it out with care.

Be present with yourself, too. Make it a habit to set aside some time every day to block off all outside distractions and just sit still by yourself. Breathe deeply, slowly let your mind drift over the day's events, and then bring it to the here and now. Stay in that perfect present for as long as you can.

"Nothing, to my way of thinking, is a better proof of a well-ordered mind than a man's ability to stop just where he is and pass some time in his own company."
Seneca, *Letters From a Stoic*

Expect To Be Challenged

"Begin each day by telling yourself: Today I shall be meeting with interference, ingratitude, insolence, disloyalty, ill-will, and selfishness - all of them due to the offenders' ignorance of what is good or evil."
Marcus Aurelius, *Meditations*

Once we remember that we have very little under our control, we must realise that we will be faced with challenges, large and small. The Stoics, being always proactive, suggest that we pre-meditate these challenges so as to prepare ourselves to face them when they happen.

Scenario 1

A woman is in a rush to process her bank transaction before her lunch hour is over. She arrives at the bank to join a long line which seems to move very slowly. The woman starts to get frustrated and takes it out on the people in front of her, clucking her tongue when she feels they're moving too slowly. When she finally arrives at the counter, she snaps at the teller to move quickly. She rushes the teller along, showing her frustration at how slowly she feels she is being served. When she receives her money, she storms out of the bank.

Scenario 2

A man is stuck in a huge traffic jam. Although he is due for a meeting, he knows that there's nothing he can do to make the traffic move faster. He calls the office to apologise for his delay and tells them to go ahead without him. He then turns up the radio and relaxes to his favourite music. While monitoring the traffic ahead, he checks his email and surfs the net for a while. He calls some of his friends to catch up. Eventually, he arrives, calm and cool, at the meeting.

The Stoic Solution

The woman in the first scenario forgot that no matter what she did or how frustrated she got, she couldn't avoid coming up against challenges. What she should have remembered is that since challenges were unavoidable, she should just relax and go with the flow. That's what the man in scenario 2 did, and he came out on top.

At the beginning of the day, spend a few moments telling yourself that today you might be cut off by a hasty driver, you might come across a surly customer service staff, or your client might be extra demanding. If the negative scenario that you've painted for yourself does occur, you won't be ruffled since you've already prepared yourself for it. If, however, you experience the opposite of what you expected - perhaps a customer service staff went out of their way to assist you - you will be happily surprised.

"There is nothing happens to any person but what was in his power to go through with."
Marcus Aurelius, Meditations

Be Uncomfortable

"Comfort is the worst kind of slavery because you're always afraid that something or someone will take it away. But if you cannot just anticipate but practice misfortune, then chance loses its ability to disrupt your life."
Seneca, Letters From a Stoic

As we've seen, Stoicism is a philosophy that advocates action. To remind you that everything in life is transient, set aside a few days every month to go without certain comforts that you've become accustomed to. During that time, put away your credit card, prepare and eat simple meals at home, set up a sleeping bag on the floor, or simplify your life in some way. At the end of the time, you will appreciate what you have.

Scenario 1

A wealthy man who jet-sets all around the world, enjoys expensive meals and parties puts aside a couple of days every month to rough it out. He throws his simplest clothes into a backpack, checks into a 1 star motel and volunteers at a homeless shelter. He cooks his own meals and cleans his own room. After a week, he comes back to his entitled life renewed in his appreciation for everything he has.

Scenario 2

After being taken for granted for many years, a disgruntled wife decides she's had enough. She gives her husband an ultimatum that he either start paying some attention to her, or she will leave. He doesn't believe her, and she actually does walk out. He finds himself at a loss, and finally realises that he made a mistake in not appreciating her.

The Stoic Solution

The wealthy man recharges his appreciation for the wonderful things that he has by reminding himself of what he could very well not have. This applies to relationships as well. Imagine your life without the people closest to you, as the man in the second scenario ended up experiencing. Examine how you would feel, what you would do, what kind of person would you be. You will then value your relationships all the more because you know that they may not always be there.

"Do not indulge in dreams of having what you have not, but reckon up the chief of the blessings you do possess, and then thankfully remember how you would crave for them if they were not yours."
Marcus Aurelius, Meditations

Mirror Image

"Choose someone whose way of life as well as words, and whose very face as mirroring the character that lies behind it, have won your approval. Be always pointing him out to yourself either as your guardian or as your model. This is a need, in my view, for someone as a standard against which our characters can measure themselves. Without a ruler to do it against you won't make the crooked straight."
Seneca, <u>Letters From a Stoic</u>

How do we inspire ourselves towards what we want to achieve? How do we know which way to go, what to do? We seek out those who show the qualities we aspire towards. Read their stories, watch documentaries on them, listen to interviews they have given, and analyse their behaviour in times of success as well as failure, as in scenario 1.

Scenario 1

When a lady feels down and out, she always takes out an autobiography about the person she looks up to and reads a couple of chapters about how they overcame adversity, how they always kept their cool in the face of negativity, and how they kept that cool, even when things went their way and they succeeded beyond their wildest dreams. The lady then grounds herself back into a logical frame of mind and carries on with her life with renewed mental strength.

Scenario 2

A teenaged boy is faced with some major decisions after graduating high school. He has been offered a good job at a respectable company but a top college has also offered him a scholarship. He doesn't know which way to go as both offers will take him places. Luckily, he knows that he can turn to his father whom he's always looked up to.

The Stoic Solution

If you're lucky enough to have someone in your life whose principles and actions speak to what you want to achieve, like the boy in scenario 2, spend as much time with them as possible. Talk to them, ask them questions, observe them, and use the time-old phrase of, "what would_____ do in this situation?" when faced with a quandary.

"Imagine for yourself a character, a model personality, whose example you determine to follow, in private as well as in public."
Epictetus, <u>Discourses</u>

Be Free Of Annoyance

"If a person gave your body to any stranger he met on his way, you would certainly be angry. And do you feel no shame in handing over your own mind to be confused and mystified by anyone who happens to verbally attack you?"
Epictetus, <u>The Enchiridion</u>

Epictetus, who was a slave for most of his young life, encourages us to remember that while our body may be enslaved, our mind is forever free. He asked - why would you allow your inherently free mind to be enslaved by annoyances, disturbances or interruptions?

Scenario 1

A woman finds a co-worker very irritating - she constantly comes over to her cubicle to ask what seem like inane questions. Over time it gets to her more and more until she cannot concentrate on her work anymore. One day she asks to be moved to another cubicle as far away from her annoyer as possible. The human resources manager finds her attitude rather negative and notes it down in her file.

Scenario 2

A girl knows that some of her classmates whisper about her behind her back because they see her as different. Day in and day out, she feels their eyes and judgements on her. At first she reacts angrily to the situation and wants to lash out at them however she comes to realise that taking that path won't change the situation, it might even provoke them further. The girl chooses to let their gossip slide off her back. She continues to smile at them and greet them normally, and she even goes out of her way to assist them when she can. Eventually, they see that she is a genuine person and they befriend her.

The Stoic Solution

Enslavement of the mind is exactly what happens when we react to 'hiccups' like those illustrated above. We can choose to get riled up, argue or prove we are right. We can choose to allow circumstances or people to annoy us, as the man in scenario 1 did. Or, we can do as the girl in scenario 2 did and not let the small stuff disturb her equilibrium. Epictetus says that reacting takes up our precious time and energy, and to what end?

"Reject your sense of injury and the injury itself disappears."
Marcus Aurelius, *Meditations*

Turn The Down Around

*"The impediment to action advances action. What stands in
the way becomes the way."*
Marcus Aurelius, *Meditations*

A few chapters ago, we discussed a lady who had faced a
disappointment. The apartment she had finally set her sights
on ended up being unavailable. She not only reacted in a level-
headed manner, she actually found a way to benefit from the
setback. She rationalised that now she could save up more and
when she finally found an apartment in the development that
she wanted, she would be more financially stable to buy it.

Scenario 2

A man is let go from his long-term job. This sends him into a
tailspin and instead of remembering how miserable he was in
the job anyway, he keeps bemoaning the fact that he's now
jobless. He keeps reminding himself that he's been out of the
market for so long that he will never find work at his level for
the pay that he was getting before. One day, he is complaining
about this to a friend who is actually just about to offer him a
job that would match all his criteria. His negative attitude
changes the friend's mind, however, and he doesn't offer him
the job.

The Stoic Solution

The difference between the lady in the aforementioned
scenario and the man in scenario 2 is that she remembered
that things aren't always as bad as they seem, whereas all he
could see was the bad. Oftentimes, we are so clouded up by

emotion when things go 'wrong' that we can't see the proverbial silver lining surrounding the dark cloud. If we kept our cool and kept looking forward instead of down, we would be able to see that most of the time, there is an opportunity lurking around to be discovered in what seems like a negative situation.

"A good person dyes events with his own colour and turns whatever happens to his own benefit."
Seneca, *Letters From a Stoic*

Practise Before You Preach

"It is difficult to bring people to goodness with lessons, but it is easy to do so by example."
Seneca, *Letters From a Stoic*

The advice to "Practise what you preach" is held in high regard in Stoic philosophy, but it's taken one step further. Stoics are encouraged to not even preach, but to show by example.

We discussed a man a while ago who was inspired by a book he had read. He took the next step to gather more knowledge and he took on the wisdom he found in those books by talking about it and sharing it, but he didn't act on it, and that is where he faltered.

Scenario 2

A volatile woman who has had many broken relationships attends a course that opens her eyes to Stoic philosophy. She vows to use the tools that she has gained to change her life. Every day she reads up on a Stoic teaching, and then she actively seeks out a situation in which to practise it. In time, her conscious efforts become second nature and her friends and family witness changes in her. She is so inspired that she trains to become a speaker, sharing about her experiences and how Stoicism can guide people to a better frame of mind.

The Stoic Solution

A Stoic is required to take personal responsibility for their thoughts, words and actions. Taking control of your thoughts, as the man in the first scenario did, is the first step, but you must carry through with it in your actions, as the lady in the second scenario did. Only then can you affect change in others around you.

"Don't explain your philosophy. Embody it."
Epictetus, Discourses

Conclusion

We can now see behind the Stoic's stoic façade to access the inner workings of what makes him so calm, so cool and collected in the face of any stimuli - positive or negative.

We have learned that the key to it all is his ability to reason - to use logic to reason that things are impermanent, uncontrollable, unstoppable, and, most importantly - mere perceptions.

Perhaps the most pertinent idea we have learned is that WE are the only constant in this mass of uncertainty and that we thankfully have full control over ourselves - our thoughts, words and deeds. Herein lies the power to overcome all obstacles, defeats and tragedies.

Along the way, we have discovered how to use logic and reason to train our thoughts, words and deeds to help us maintain a sense of equilibrium. We have learned not to allow external forces to affect us and steer us away from our pursuit of logic. We have learned to keep emotions in check so that they do not tip the boat. We have learned to stay present and focused and realised that ownership is a myth and that letting go is natural.

Now that we have some powerful Stoic tools with which to tackle this thing called life and all its foibles, we must remember what Epictetus said, *"The first and most important topic in philosophy is the practical application of principles."*

As with anything in life, we must now pick and choose what aspects of this powerful philosophy we can apply to our daily lives to enrich it. And then we must live it.

"While you live, while it is in your power, be good."
Marcus Aurelius

Made in the USA
Lexington, KY
21 October 2017